BAR·B·Q

Written by Christine Smith

TOP THAT!™

Copyright © 2004 Top That! Publishing plc,
Top That! Publishing, 27023 McBean Parkway, #408 Valencia, CA 91355
www.topthatpublishing.com

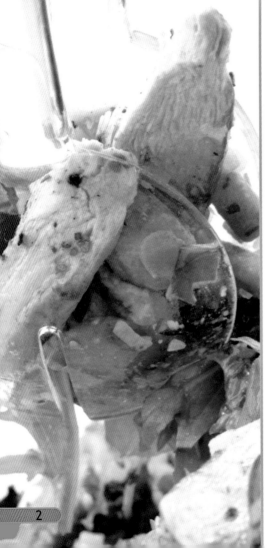

Contents

⊙ BREADS AND SALADS

⊙ STARTERS

⊙ BEEF

Introduction

All over the world people cook on open fires—whether it be a few sticks in a Greek village courtyard burning to provide the heat to cook deep-fried pastries, a brazier on a French street market char-grilling pieces of eel, or even a charcoal fire in half an oil drum cooking succulent meat and vegetable kebabs in North Africa. This is the way cooking started and today, despite being basic, it is becoming more and more popular. Cooking on an open fire is simple, effective, and produces wonderful food with minimum fuss and maximum flavor. Cooking outside is great in hot weather when no one wants to be stuck indoors over a hot stove. It lends itself to relaxed al fresco eating with friends and family as everyone is usually drawn to the barbecue and can take part in the preparation and cooking. Barbecue parties are great fun, and are synonymous with easy, summer entertaining.

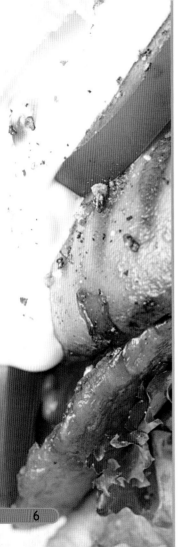

Building Your Own Barbecue

Whatever type of barbecue you decide to use, the principles are the same. Food is put on a wire rack above a source of heat. As the food cooks, juices, fat, and moisture drip off onto the heat and this creates moist smoke which then rises up to flavor the food. There are numerous types of barbecues available to buy, from simple, disposable ones, ideal for an instant picnic, to elaborate, expensive gas-fired barbecues. In deciding the type you want you need to think about how often you are likely to want to cook outside, how many people you are likely to be catering for, and where you will usually want to cook—at home or when out on trips and picnics.

Kits

⊙ If you are likely to have regular barbecues at home for family and friends you may want to build your own permanent barbecue rather than buy a ready-made one, especially if you really like the idea of getting into cooking outside. Kits can be bought at hardware stores with all the necessary parts to build the barbecue, or you can just use ordinary house bricks with fire bricks inside for durability.

Choose your spot carefully in the yard—it needs to be sheltered, not too far from the kitchen and near where people will be able to sit and eat food straight from the grill. For a really efficient outside cooking operation, adjoining surfaces to work on and an outside sink are useful.

Building a Simple Barbecue

⊙ For the most basic of barbecues, just put a few stones together in a circle, place a piece of chicken wire or simple grid on top and add the fuel in the center of the stones. If you want to make a more regular structure add bricks. Both can be put together and dismantled quickly and easily and require little planning or resources.

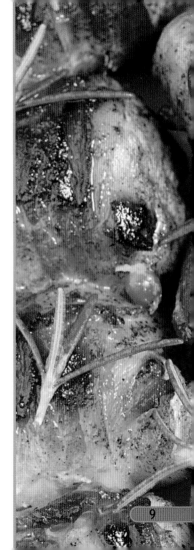

Choosing Your Barbecue

Disposables

⊙ The cheapest type of barbecue you can buy is a disposable one consisting of a tinfoil tray, a wire rack to fit over the top, and a small amount of charcoal. These are ideal for a quick picnic or seaside cooking session, as they are easy to transport and can be thrown away afterward. Of course, you can easily make your own version. Punch a few holes in a large cookie tin, fill with some charcoal and put a simple wire rack or piece of chicken wire on top. If you are on the beach you could use driftwood or some sticks as fuel.

Hibachis

⊙ Charcoal barbecues vary in size. The small hibachi is a shallow, steel, aluminum or cast-iron barbecue with an adjustable air hole in the base and a wire rack on top which can be fitted into notches at various heights over the charcoal. Available in single or double size, it is ideal for cooking smaller pieces of food such as kebabs. As hibachis sit on very small legs, they are stable and can be used either on the ground or on the table on top of a heatproof surface. Choose a cast-iron hibachi for durability and heat retention, but bear in mind that steel or aluminum versions will be cheaper and lightweight to transport. Of course, there are all sorts of barbecues on longer legs which are easier to cook on because they are at standing height.

Cast-iron Potbellied Barbecues

⊙ Another good, attractive barbecue, that has recently become widely available at a very reasonable price, is a cast-iron potbellied barbecue on short legs. These are usually not too big, yet combine many of the features of more expensive models. They are made from a casting which makes them very stable and are able to reach the temperature for cooking quickly. Another feature available is an electric, or battery-operated, spit. This can be very useful for cooking larger pieces of meat evenly without burning.

Kettle Barbecues

⊙ Some models have hinged lids to put over the food as it is cooking. These lids work as wind breaks and also help to keep cooked food warm. Some larger versions, often called kettle barbecues because of their shape, can be used to cook whole joints of meat quite successfully as the lid helps to deflect heat and brown the meat on all sides. You can also use this type of barbecue to smoke food at home as it holds the smoke within the body of the stove.

Gas Barbecues

◉ Gas barbecues, which use gas to heat lava rocks or flat bars, have lots of advantages—they are clean, easy and quick to light, and are ready for cooking much more quickly than a charcoal stove. The temperature is also much easier to control. Food has a good flavor as the juices from the cooking food drip on to the hot rocks or surface, evaporate, and flavor the food just as in a charcoal barbecue.

Check on the efficiency of the model you are considering—some do use a lot of gas very quickly. Also look at the ignition system and its ease of use.

The obvious disadvantage of a gas barbecue is the cost of purchase. They also tend to be rather large to store when not in use.

Beehives

◉ Beehive ovens are a more permanent type of outside cooker. Especially good for cooking bread and pizzas on their hot floor, they will also keep everyone warm on a cold evening.

A beehive oven is usually fixed permanently onto an outside area. Once again, it is worth ensuring that you have working areas on either side in order to make cooking simple and straightforward.

The Cooking Area

One important factor to consider, whatever type of barbecue you choose, is the size of the cooking area. Make sure that you will have enough space to cook the type of food you want. Some barbecue models also incorporate warming racks which sit above the cooking grill. These may seem a good idea but can get in the way and be a hindrance to easy cooking. Shelves attached to the sides of the cooking area, however, can be useful for putting tools down.

The Fire

A good barbecue is only as good as the fire you make. Lighting and maintaining the fire at the right temperature comes with practice. There are lots of different types of fuel you can use, although obviously if you are using a gas barbecue all you will need is a gas cylinder.

Wood

⊙ Hardwoods like oak or olive wood burn slowly and create an aromatic smoke for cooking food. However, wood fires can be difficult to light and do not produce as even or long-lasting a heat as charcoal. Kindling wood is very useful for starting a charcoal fire.

Charcoal

⊙ There are two main types of charcoal: lump wood and briquettes. Lump wood charcoal is produced by firing softwood in a kiln. Lump wood charcoal is easier to light than briquettes but does not burn for as long. Buy good-quality charcoal— preferably produced according to sustainability standards, as widespread charcoal production has contributed to deforestation in tropical rainforests.

Briquettes are processed from charcoal and, although more difficult to light, do burn for longer than lump wood charcoal. You can buy self-lighting charcoal which has been impregnated with a lighting fluid. When using this or any other lighting agent it is very important to make sure that all the lighting agent has burnt off before putting the food on the grill.

Lighting the Fire

⊙ If you want to use them, lighting fluids are available which will make lighting the charcoal, whether lump wood or briquettes, much easier. However, as with self-lighting charcoal, you must wait until all the fluid has been burnt off before cooking as the smell could taint the food. You can also use special barbecue fire lighters in the base of the fire to help get the charcoal alight.

It is relatively easy to light the charcoal using newspaper and pieces of kindling wood. Twist up two or three sheets of newspaper tightly and place in a pyramid at the base of the barbecue. Build a small tower with six or seven pieces of kindling wood. Put some pieces of charcoal in amongst the paper and wood and then light the paper. Once the charcoal has started to burn and glow red, spread it out, adding more pieces as the heat builds up to create an even fire.

You can also buy little metal chimney structures which you can use in the center of the barbecue to create a hot base for the fire. This should be removed before adding more charcoal.

The Principle

⊙ Whichever method you use to get the charcoal alight, do not be tempted to fill the barbecue with too much charcoal at the beginning. The principle is to get a small amount of charcoal burning before gradually adding more. It is harder to increase the heat of a barbecue fire than it is to reduce it so before cooking ensure that you have more charcoal on the barbecue than you might need, as it can then be left to burn down, if too hot.

The glowing charcoal is then left for some time to allow it to get up to temperature—anything up to 40 minutes. When the flames have disappeared and the charcoal is glowing and covered with white ash the fire is ready.

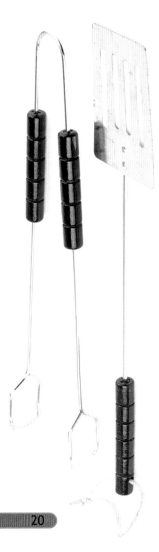

Tools

Apart from choosing the right sort of barbecue to suit your

needs you can have a lot of fun collecting together pieces of

equipment and tools to help you with the cooking.

⊙ Wire racks are great if you have food such as a whole fish, a piece of meat, or even burgers and sausages that you want to turn once or more during cooking.

⊙ Long-handled tongs are essential for lifting food on and off the hot grill.

⊙ A long-handled bristle brush is useful for basting the food as it is cooking.

⊙ A long-handled metal spatula and fork are good for turning items on the rack.

⊙ Different skewers—use long, flat, metal ones for chunks of meat and fish, and wooden ones for smaller items that cook more quickly.

⊙ A meat thermometer is really useful, especially when cooking larger pieces of pork or chicken where it is essential that the meat is cooked through properly.

Cooking on a Barbecue

The key to success when cooking on a barbecue is to be organized. Get everything ready in good time. Once the fire is ready for cooking on, you should be ready to cook and serve the food. Lots of food cooks quite quickly so have everything ready at the start.

Getting the Temperature Right

⊙ There is a simple way to ascertain the temperature of the fire. Simply hold your hand about 10 in./25 cm away from the charcoal and, if you can keep your hand there for:

2 seconds, the fire is hot;
4-5 seconds, the fire is medium hot;
5-6 seconds, the fire is medium;
7-8 seconds, the fire is cool.

Also, as the fire cools down the coals become whiter and covered with thick layers of ash.

Adjusting the Temperature of the Fire

⊙ Some food, for example, thin pieces of meat and fish, can be cooked quickly at a hot temperature, whereas kebabs, vegetables and thicker pieces of meat, such as chicken, joints etc., will need longer at a medium heat. Achieving different temperatures for the fire is therefore useful. The simplest way is to move the food nearer or further away from the fire according to the temperature that you need. However, you can also increase the temperature slightly by pushing the charcoal together, blowing off some of the ash and opening any air vents. Conversely, you can reduce the temperature by spreading out the coals and closing any air vents.

It is possible to cook foods needing different temperatures at the same time by placing some food directly over the hot charcoal and putting food that needs slower cooking at the side of the cooking area.

Direct Grilling

⊙ Direct grilling involves putting the food straight above the heat on the rack. The food cooks fairly quickly and you will need to turn it to cook it on all sides.

Indirect Grilling

⊙ You can also cook on a barbecue using indirect heat. This is especially suitable for larger pieces of meat, where a gentler heat is needed to penetrate the food and cook it through without burning the outside. To cook in this way you need a barbecue with a lid. Keep the heat to the sides of the barbecue and put the food into the center with a drip tray underneath. Cover the barbecue with the lid which then reflects heat to cook the food from all sides. Do not lift the lid too often as the accumulated heat will escape. The barbecue works as a conventional oven and the food becomes flavorsome and moist because the juices evaporate to permeate the food.

Kebabs

⊙ Do not thread food onto kebabs too tightly—cooking will take much longer if the pieces of food are very close together, and the outside will burn before the inside is cooked.

Skewers

Soak wooden skewers in water for thirty minutes before use to prevent them from becoming scorched.

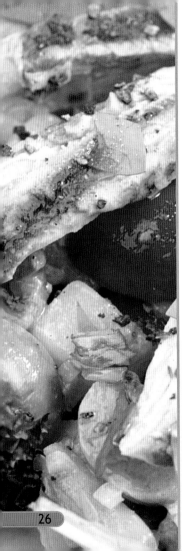

Cooking Times

Cooking on a barbecue is rather more art than science as the heat of the fire is affected by many factors: size, wind, type of fuel, and type of barbecue. The length of time it takes to cook particular food can also be affected by, for example, the thickness of a piece of meat or how much is put on the grill at the same time. However, it is still helpful to have a rough idea of the average cooking time. Just as you should make sure that meats such as chicken and pork are cooked all the way through, it is also important to avoid overcooking foods like fish, thereby spoiling the flavor and texture.

Chicken

⊙ Chicken must always be cooked thoroughly. One trick is to cook joints in a microwave or conventional oven first, just finishing off the cooking on the barbecue. Fifteen to twenty minutes at 392°F (200°C) in a conventional oven will reduce the time on the barbecue by about ten minutes, and ensure that the inside of the chicken is cooked without the outside becoming too scorched. Chicken breasts are easily cooked on the barbecue, especially if they are flattened out before cooking, slashed, or cut into smaller pieces as in kebabs. Chicken is best cooked over a medium heat. Such lean meat needs to be brushed with olive oil to keep it moist during cooking. The chicken is cooked when all signs of pinkness have gone and any juices run clear.

> APPROXIMATE COOKING TIMES
> Whole chicken on a spit: 1-1^1/$_2$ hours
> Chicken quarters: 30 minutes
> Drumsticks or thighs: 25 minutes
> Whole boneless breasts: 15 minutes
> Kebabs: 10 minutes
> Spatchcocked poussin: 30 minutes

Lamb

⊙ Lamb is the perfect meat to grill on the barbecue as its proportion of fat keeps the meat moist and full of flavor. Lamb can either be cooked all the way through or left a little pink in the middle, according to taste. A leg of lamb or even a whole lamb cooked on a spit over charcoal is wonderful, and is, of course, reminiscent of much outdoor cooking in the area around the Mediterranean.

Always leave a joint of lamb to rest, covered in tinfoil, before carving—this allows the meat to settle and become more tender. Cook smaller pieces of lamb over a medium heat. Check cooking progress by using a meat thermometer inserted into the center of the meat—170°F (75°C) indicates the lamb is well cooked, 150°F (65°C) that it is rare.

APPROXIMATE COOKING TIMES
Chops: 15 minutes
Leg steaks: 15 minutes
Kebabs: 10-15 minutes
Boned leg of lamb: 45-60 minutes

Pork

⊙ Pork can be quite lean so make sure you baste it well during cooking to keep it moist. Like chicken, it is important to cook the pork all the way through. To make this easier, cut the meat into smaller pieces—pork makes wonderful kebabs. Leave a larger piece to rest for a few minutes covered with tinfoil before serving. Sausages are excellent on the barbecue and usually have enough fat content to keep them moist. Pork should be cooked over a medium heat to ensure the inside is cooked without burning the outside.

APPROXIMATE COOKING TIMES
Chops: 15 minutes
Steaks: 15 minutes
Kebabs: 15 minutes
Sausages (depending on thickness): 6-10 minutes

Beef

⊙ Steaks on the grill are a simple, yet superb, way of enjoying beef. Choose beef that is marbled with fat to ensure good flavor and moistness. Rump or sirloin should be cooked quickly at a high temperature to achieve succulence. Home-made beefburgers made from lean minced beef are also excellent on the barbecue and always popular.

APPROXIMATE COOKING TIMES
Steaks (depending on thickness)
rare: 5 minutes
medium: 8 minutes
well done: 10-12 minutes
Burgers (depending on thickness): 5-8 minutes

Fish

 Salmon, mackerel, herring, and tuna work really well on the grill as their oiliness keeps them moist. White fish such as cod or haddock can become dry if grilled on the barbecue unless well basted with an oily marinade. Choose firm-textured white fish such as monkfish for best results. Both monkfish and salmon are firm enough to be used for kebabs. Take care not to overcook fish as the texture and flavor will be spoiled. The fish is cooked when the flesh becomes opaque. Keep the skin on the fish while cooking—it helps with turning the fish during cooking and stops it breaking up.

APPROXIMATE COOKING TIMES
Whole fish
Large (depending on thickness):
10-15 minutes over a medium heat
Small (depending on size and thickness):
6-10 minutes over a high heat
Steaks and fillets:
7-10 minutes over a medium heat
Kebabs: 5-7 minutes

Achieving Flavor

There are three ways to flavor your barbecued food.

Before Cooking

◉ Most food benefits from marinating before cooking. A liquid marinade based on olive oil, lemon juice, yogurt, herbs, or spices will enhance the flavor and texture of most food. When marinating meat, do not add salt to the marinade as this will draw out the natural juices in the meat, making it dry and tough. Lamb and beef can be marinated for several hours, while the leaner meats of pork and chicken should only be marinated for two hours at most, otherwise the meat will dry out. Fish also benefits from being marinated but needs only one or two hours as it absorbs flavors quickly. Vegetables can also be marinated, with mushrooms in particular benefiting.

Another way to flavor food before cooking is to rub in a dry mixture of herbs and/or spices. Cover and leave in a cool place for one or two hours. Brush off the excess, brush with oil and grill as normal.

During Cooking

⊙ Basting meat, fish, and vegetables during cooking keeps the food moist and will also add flavor. When you make the marinade, keep a little to one side before putting the rest over the food. Use this marinade for basting while cooking. Do not use marinade that you have drained from the food as you may contaminate food that is nearly cooked with marinade that has been on uncooked food. Alternatively, baste with extra olive oil mixed with a little lemon juice. Fresh herbs such as rosemary can be sprinkled over the food for extra flavor. Towards the end of cooking you can brush the food with a glaze, perhaps made with honey. A few minutes of heat will turn this into a rich, sticky coating. This is really good for sticky ribs, belly pork or sausages. At the end of cooking, season with salt.

Another way to flavor food as it is cooking is to put some branches of rosemary, vine prunings or other aromatics like hickory wood onto the hot charcoal, and the aromas will drift up to flavor the food.

After Cooking

⊙ An excellent way to flavor all barbecued food once it is cooked is to add a little butter or oil flavored with herbs or spices. This will melt over the hot food, coating it in a lovely flavored mixture. You can, of course, just sprinkle the cooked food with herbs, spices, salt, and pepper.

Safety Tips

- ⊙ Make sure your barbecue is level, safe, and stable.

- ⊙ Only use barbecue lighting fluids and agents with your charcoal, and always follow the instructions carefully.

- ⊙ Long-handled tools and oven gloves help prevent burns and other minor accidents.

- ⊙ Keep raw and cooked food separately, with raw meat in covered containers in a cooler, especially if it is a hot day.

- ⊙ Cut off extra fat from meat—too much fat or oil can make the charcoal flare up. Keep a bottle of spray water to hand —a quick spray will put out any unwelcome flames.

- ⊙ Make sure chicken and pork are cooked through—test with a skewer to make sure the juices run clear, or use a meat thermometer.

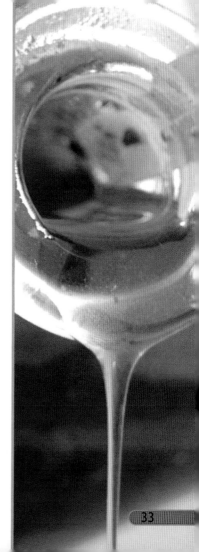

Focaccia Bread

FOR THE BREAD:
- 1 lb 2 oz/500 g semolina flour
- 1 lb 2 oz/500 g pasta flour
- 8½ fl oz/250 ml olive oil
- 1 oz/30 g yeast or ¼ oz/3 x 7 g sachets of dried yeast
- 1 pint/570 ml warm water
- 1 tbsp honey, to help yeast

FOR THE TOPPING:
- 2 punnets of cherry vine tomatoes
- 2 cloves of garlic
- 3 potatoes, cooked, cooled, and sliced
- medium bunch fresh thyme, picked and chopped
- medium bunch fresh rosemary, picked and chopped
- olive oil, to drizzle on top

⊙ SERVES 4 ⊙ PREPARATION TIME: 30-60 minutes ⊙ COOKING TIME: 10-30 minutes

⊙ COST: Low DIFFICULTY: Easy

1. Put the warm water in a large bowl, add the semolina flour and work into a porridge-like consistency. Then mix in the yeast, olive oil, honey, and finally the pasta flour. Knead until smooth, cut in half and leave for 10-15 minutes.

2. Rinse the tomatoes and peel and loosely crush the garlic.

3. Dust a board with semolina flour and roll out each half of dough to 1 in./2.5 cm thickness.

4. Using your thumbs, push the tomatoes, half the garlic and the thyme into one half of the bread. On the other half push the potatoes, garlic, and rosemary into the dough. Prove until they have doubled in size.

5. Place in a preheated oven (350°F/180°C/Gas 4) for 30 minutes. When ready, take the bread out of the oven, drizzle olive oil over the top and serve.

Garlic Bread

⊙ SERVES
4-6

⊙ PREPARATION TIME:
20 minutes

⊙ COST:
Low

⊙ COOKING TIME:
5-10 minutes

DIFFICULTY:
Very easy

INGREDIENTS

⊙ 1 baguette
⊙ 3 cloves of smoked or ordinary garlic
⊙ salt
⊙ olive oil
⊙ 4 oz/125 g butter

1. Preheat the oven to its highest temperature.
2. Crush the cloves of garlic and mix in with the butter.
3. Slice the bread so that the knife doesn't go all the way through. Each section should be about 1 in./2.5 cm thick.
4. Open a section at a time and spread the garlic butter inside the bread. Drizzle with olive oil and season with salt.
5. Place the baguette on a tray and put in the oven for 5-10 minutes. When ready, take out and serve.

Crisp Green Salad

- 1 little gem, frisée and lollo bionda lettuce
- 3 sticks of celery
- 6 green onions
- ½ cucumber
- salad croutons
- 1 bunch of chives

FOR THE DRESSING:
- 2 tbsp extra virgin olive oil
- ½ tsp cider vinegar
- 1 tsp balsamic vinegar
- 1 tsp lemon juice
- a dash of Worcestershire sauce
- salt and freshly ground black pepper

⊙ SERVES 4   ⊙ PREPARATION TIME: ⊙ COOKING TIME:
                 15 minutes   None
               ⊙ COST: DIFFICULTY:
                 Low   Easy

1. Wash and dry the lettuce, then roughly tear up the lettuce leaves. Put the leaves in a salad bowl and leave to one side.
2. Now chop the celery and green onions and toss into the lettuce leaves.
3. Quarter and slice the cucumber and sprinkle over the top of the salad.
4. Whisk together the olive oil, cider and balsamic vinegar, lemon juice, Worcestershire sauce, and salt and pepper in a small bowl. Pour the dressing over the salad, coating well.
5. Sprinkle over the croutons and some chopped chives to finish.

Tomato and Mozzarella Salad

⊙ SERVES 4   ⊙ PREPARATION TIME: 10 minutes   ⊙ COOKING TIME: None

⊙ COST: Low   ⊙ DIFFICULTY: Easy

INGREDIENTS

- ⊙ 4 beefsteak tomatoes
- ⊙ 1 lb 4 oz/600 g of mozzarella cheese
- ⊙ 1 bunch basil leaves
- ⊙ coarse ground black pepper
- ⊙ extra virgin olive oil

1. Slice the tops off the tomatoes and then slice the rest of the tomatoes and mozzarella into even-sized pieces.
2. Lay slices of tomato alternately over slices of mozzarella on each person's plate.
3. Tear the basil leaves and sprinkle over the top of the salad.
4. Drizzle olive oil over the top of the salad, then sprinkle on the pepper to finish.

Asparagus Wrapped in Pancetta

- ⊙ 1 lb 2 oz/500 g
  thin asparagus
- ⊙ a few sprigs
  fresh rosemary
- ⊙ shavings of
  Parmesan cheese
- ⊙ 8-10 strips of pancetta
  or thinly sliced
  unsmoked streaky bacon
- ⊙ olive oil
- ⊙ freshly ground
  black pepper

⊙ SERVES 4 ⊙ PREPARATION TIME: ⊙ COOKING TIME:
10 minutes   4-5 minutes
⊙ COST: DIFFICULTY:
Low   Easy

1. Trim the asparagus and divide into eight bundles. Put one or
   two Parmesan shavings and rosemary sprigs into each bundle.
2. Carefully wrap each bundle with the strips of pancetta or
   streaky bacon, making sure the bundles are secure.
   Brush each bundle with a little olive oil and season with
   black pepper.
3. Cook on a hot barbecue for 4-5 minutes, turning to brown
   on all sides.

Sweet Corn with Garlic Butter

⊙ SERVES 4   ⊙ PREPARATION TIME: ⊙ COOKING TIME:
                    10 minutes   15-20 minutes
             ⊙ COST: DIFFICULTY:
                    Very low   Very easy

⊙ 4 cobs of sweet corn
⊙ 3 oz/75 g melted
   unsalted butter
⊙ 2 cloves of garlic, crushed
⊙ juice of ½ a lemon
⊙ freshly ground
   black pepper
⊙ crushed sea salt

1. Trim the husks and silks from the sweet corn. Brush each
   cob with melted butter and grill gently on the barbecue
   for 15-20 minutes, until the kernels are slightly brown
   and tender.

2. Meanwhile, mix the rest of the butter with the crushed
   garlic and lemon juice. When the sweet corn is cooked
   sprinkle with the black pepper and salt.

3. Serve with the garlic butter on the side.

Sweet and Sour Grilled Peppers

- 3 red peppers
- 3 yellow or orange peppers
- 2 tbsp olive oil
- 1 tbsp cider vinegar
- 1 tsp sugar
- 1 small red onion, very finely chopped
- 4 oz/125 g sweet cherry tomatoes, finely diced
- 2 tbsp fresh coriander, finely chopped
- salt and freshly ground black pepper

⊙ SERVES 4 ⊙ PREPARATION TIME:
5 minutes

⊙ COOKING TIME:
15 minutes

⊙ COST:
Low

DIFFICULTY:
Fairly easy

1. Cook the whole peppers on the barbecue for fifteen minutes, turning several times. The skin should be blackened and blistered. Set aside to cool, covering with a dish towel.

2. Mix all the rest of the ingredients together in a bowl. When the peppers are cool, carefully peel the skin, remove the seeds and stalk, and cut into thick slices. Mix with the olive oil mixture and serve on a shallow dish. If you like, use chunks of crusty bread to soak up the juices.

Basil Prawns

⊙ SERVES 4   ⊙ PREPARATION TIME: ⊙ COOKING TIME:
                 1 hour 10 minutes   4-6 minutes

             ⊙ COST: DIFFICULTY:
             Low   Very easy

1. Place the olive oil, melted butter, lemon juice, mustard, basil, garlic, and salt and pepper in a shallow dish and mix until the ingredients are blended together. Add the prawns, coating them in the mix. Cover and refrigerate for an hour.

2. Remove the prawns from the marinade and thread on skewers. Cook over medium coals for 2-3 minutes on each side, basting with any remaining marinade from time to time. Serve immediately.

INGREDIENTS

- ⊙ 12 large tiger prawns, peeled and de-veined
- ⊙ 2 tbsp Dijon mustard
- ⊙ 2 oz/50 g melted butter
- ⊙ 3 garlic cloves, crushed
- ⊙ 2 tbsp olive oil
- ⊙ 2 tbsp freshly chopped basil leaves
- ⊙ juice of one large lemon
- ⊙ salt and white pepper

Spicy Chicken Wings

- 6-8 chicken wings
- creole seasoning

FOR THE MARINADE:
- juice of 1-2 lemons
- 1 small onion, grated
- 3 garlic cloves, crushed
- 1/2 tsp ground cumin
- 1 tbsp ginger syrup
- 1/4 tsp ground cinnamon
- 1/4 tsp cayenne pepper
- 1 tbsp vegetable oil

- SERVES 4
- PREPARATION TIME: 2 hours 10 minutes
- COST: Reasonable
- COOKING TIME: 20 minutes
- DIFFICULTY: Very easy

1. Remove the wing tips from the chicken wings and cut each in half at the joint.

2. Mix together the marinade ingredients in a bowl until they are thoroughly blended together.

3. Pour the marinade over the chicken, cover, and leave to marinate for two hours.

4. Remove the chicken from the marinade, sprinkle with the creole seasoning, then cook over hot coals, turning and basting with the marinade frequently for twenty minutes or until cooked through.

Italian Meatballs with Rich Tomato Sauce

⊙ SERVES 4 ⊙ PREPARATION TIME: 20 minutes ⊙ COOKING TIME: 15 minutes

⊙ COST: Reasonable ⊙ DIFFICULTY: Average

1. Put all the ingredients for the meatballs into a large bowl. Mix well and then, using your hands, shape into small balls. Cover with plastic wrap and set aside in the fridge.

2. Put some oil into a large saucepan and then melt the butter into it over a medium heat. Add the onion and garlic and cook until the sauce is soft and golden. Add the tomatoes, oregano, and water and cook for ten minutes. Add the sugar, milk, salt and black pepper. Continue to cook for another five minutes. Keep the sauce warm until the meatballs are ready.

3. Brush the meatballs with olive oil and cook for 8-10 minutes over a medium heat, turning to brown on all sides. Put into a serving dish, pour over the hot tomato sauce and serve.

INGREDIENTS

FOR THE MEATBALLS:
- ⊙ 1 lb 2 oz/500 g lean minced beef
- ⊙ 1 oz/25 g grated Parmesan cheese
- ⊙ 2 cloves of garlic, crushed
- ⊙ 1 tsp dried basil
- ⊙ 2 tbsp chopped parsley
- ⊙ 1 oz /25 g breadcrumbs
- ⊙ 1 egg, beaten
- ⊙ salt and black pepper
- ⊙ olive oil

FOR THE SAUCE:
- ⊙ 1 oz/25 g butter
- ⊙ 1 tbsp olive oil
- ⊙ 1 onion, finely chopped
- ⊙ 1 clove of garlic, crushed
- ⊙ 1 tin chopped tomatoes
- ⊙ 1 tsp dried oregano
- ⊙ 6 ½ tbsp/100 ml water
- ⊙ ½ tsp sugar
- ⊙ 4 tbsp milk
- ⊙ salt and black pepper

- 3 tbsp mayonnaise
- 1 tbsp natural yogurt
- 2 tsp whole grain mustard
- 4 5 oz/150 g sirloin steaks
- olive oil
- freshly ground black pepper
- 4 large floury buns
- unsalted butter
- 1 small red onion, sliced into very fine rings
- 4 tomatoes sliced
- 1 small cos lettuce, cut into fine strips
- a few sprigs of watercress
- salt and freshly ground black pepper

Sirloin Steak Sandwiches with Mustard Mayonnaise

- SERVES 4
- PREPARATION TIME: 5 minutes
- COOKING TIME: 6-12 minutes
- COST: Reasonable
- DIFFICULTY: Very easy

1. Mix together the mayonnaise, yogurt, and whole grain mustard.
2. Brush the steaks with olive oil and sprinkle with black pepper. Cook the steaks on a medium heat for 3-6 minutes on each side, turning once. The time depends on how well done you would like the steaks.
3. Butter the buns and put the steaks onto the bottom halves. Top with rings of onion, tomato slices, lettuce, and watercress. Season with salt and black pepper and drizzle with a little olive oil. Cover with the tops of the buns and serve with the mustard mayonnaise on the side.

Tuscan Steak with Sun-dried Tomato Marinade

⊙ SERVES 2 ⊙ PREPARATION TIME: ⊙ COOKING TIME:
2 hours 15 minutes 6-10 minutes

⊙ COST: ⊙ DIFFICULTY:
Average Medium

1. Mix the wine, sun-dried tomatoes, basil leaves, olive oil, garlic, salt, and pepper together until you have a smooth, thick sauce. Pour into a shallow baking dish.

2. Add steaks and turn until evenly coated. Cover and place in a refrigerator for two hours.

3. Remove the steaks from the marinade and grill on a high heat until they are done. Discard the marinade.

⊙ 2 top rump steaks
1 in./2.5 cm thick
⊙ 4 fl oz/125 ml red wine
⊙ 8-10 sun-dried tomatoes
packed in oil, drained
⊙ a handful of fresh
basil leaves
⊙ 3 tbsp olive oil
⊙ 4 cloves of garlic,
chopped
⊙ 2 tsp fresh ground
black pepper
⊙ 1 tsp salt

- 1 lb 6 oz/680 g raw hamburger meat
- 1 finely diced onion
- ½ tsp salt
- ⅛ tsp pepper
- 2 tbsp butter or margarine
- 8 oz/225 g sliced mushrooms
- 6 slices cheddar cheese

Mushroom Stuffed Burgers

⊙ SERVES 6   ⊙ PREPARATION TIME: ⊙ COOKING TIME:
            15 minutes   4-6 minutes
            ⊙ COST: DIFFICULTY:
            Low   Easy

1. Combine the hamburger meat, onion, salt, and pepper. Mix well.

2. Sauté the mushrooms in butter until they have softened and are slightly brown.

3. Form the meat mixture into twelve patties, each about ¼ in./1 cm thick. Spoon about one-sixth of the mushrooms onto six of the patties. Top each one with cheese and a second patty.

4. Seal around the edges, making sure that the patties are solid. Place on a preheated grill and cook for a couple of minutes per side. Remove when done and serve.

Char-grilled Chicken Sandwiches

⊙ SERVES 6 ⊙ PREPARATION TIME: ⊙ COOKING TIME:
2 hours 10 minutes 10-12 minutes

⊙ COST: DIFFICULTY:
Reasonable Average

1. Pound the chicken breasts until they are 1 in./2.5 cm
   in thickness. Cut each breast into two equal-sized pieces.
   Coat the chicken breasts in a mixture of three tablespoons
   of olive oil, black pepper, and thyme leaves. Cover and
   refrigerate for two hours.

2. Meanwhile, cut the bell peppers into quarters and lightly
   coat with the remaining olive oil. Place on the barbecue and
   cook until the surface begins to char. Turn to heat evenly.

3. Remove the peppers from the barbecue and cut into thin
   slices. Combine mayonnaise, mustard, Worcestershire sauce,
   red wine vinegar, and salt in a non-reactive container.

4. Cook the chicken breasts on the barbecue for 5-6 minutes
   per side. Remove from the barbecue, allowing the juices to
   run clear.

5. Add the roasted peppers and sauce and assemble with the
   rocket leaves and tomatoes into buns or sandwiches.

INGREDIENTS

⊙ 3 skinless, boneless
chicken breasts
⊙ 2 red bell peppers
⊙ 3 tomatoes, sliced
⊙ 3 oz/85 g rocket leaves
⊙ 4 tbsp mayonnaise
⊙ 2 tbsp Dijon-style
mustard
⊙ 5 tbsp olive oil
⊙ 2 tbsp fresh thyme
⊙ 1 tbsp black pepper
⊙ 1 tsp Worcestershire
sauce
⊙ 1 tsp red wine vinegar
⊙ 1 tsp salt
⊙ 6 buns or 12 slices
of bread

Chicken Kebabs

- 8 oz/225 g chicken breast skinned and boned
- 2 tbsp olive oil
- 1 tbsp lemon juice
- 1 clove of garlic, crushed
- a few sprigs of rosemary, finely chopped
- ½ tsp dried oregano
- salt and freshly ground black pepper
- 8-12 cherry tomatoes
- 2 small green peppers
- 2 baby zucchinis
- extra olive oil for basting
- metal skewers or wooden skewers, soaked in water for 30 minutes

SERVES	PREPARATION TIME:	COOKING TIME:
4-6	2 hours	10 minutes
	COST:	DIFFICULTY:
	Reasonable	Average

1. Cut the breast meat into chunks 1 in./2.5 cm square. Whisk together the olive oil, lemon juice, garlic, rosemary, oregano, and salt and pepper in a large bowl. Add the chicken breast, coating well. Cover the bowl and put in the fridge for two hours.

2. Cut the tomatoes in half if large, keep whole if small. Cut the peppers into small chunks and the zucchinis into slices.

3. Drain the chicken, reserving the marinade. Thread the chicken onto the skewers, alternating with the tomatoes, peppers, and zucchinis. Brush each kebab with the reserved marinade and cook on a medium barbecue for ten minutes, basting the kebabs regularly with a little extra olive oil and turning to ensure even cooking.

Poussin with Five Spices and Honey

⊙ SERVES 4   ⊙ PREPARATION TIME: ⊙ COOKING TIME:
                  3 hours   20-25 minutes
              ⊙ COST: DIFFICULTY:
                  Reasonable   Average

1. Prepare the poussins by flattening them on a chopping board, breast side up, to break the breast bone. Turn over, cut down each side of the backbone, remove it and cut each poussin in half. Place in a shallow dish.

2. Put the spices into a grinder and process into a powder. Add the garlic, honey, olive oil, and soy sauce. Pour over the poussins and rub into the skins. Cover with plastic wrap, put into the fridge and leave for two hours.

3. Remove the poussins from the marinade and cook on a hot barbecue for 20-25 minutes, brushing with a little extra honey and turning occasionally while cooking. Make sure that the poussins are well cooked without any trace of pink in the flesh.

INGREDIENTS

⊙ 4 poussins, about
  1 lb/450 g each

FOR THE
FIVE SPICE MIXTURE:
⊙ 1 star anise
⊙ 1 tsp fennel seed
⊙ 1 tsp coriander seed
⊙ 1 tsp Sichuan pepper
⊙ 2 cloves of garlic
⊙ 4 tbsp clear honey
⊙ 2 tbsp olive oil
⊙ 2 tbsp soy sauce

Mediterranean Grilled Chicken Salad

⊙ SERVES 4 ⊙ PREPARATION TIME: ⊙ COOKING TIME:
10 minutes 20-30 minutes

⊙ COST: DIFFICULTY:
Low Quite easy

FOR THE VINAIGRETTE:
- 4 fl oz/125 ml olive oil
- 2 fl oz/60 ml white wine vinegar
- 1½ tbsp Dijon mustard
- 1 tbsp fresh tarragon chopped (or 1½ tsp dried tarragon)
- 2 cloves of garlic minced
- ½ tsp sugar
- ½ tsp salt
- ¼ tsp black pepper

FOR THE SALAD:
- 4 skinless, boneless chicken breasts
- 4 medium potatoes, cut into small cubes
- 12 small mushrooms, halved
- handful green beans, cut into 1 in./2.5 cm pieces
- ½ red onion, chopped
- 8 cherry tomatoes, halved

1. Boil the potatoes for 10-15 minutes, until tender.
2. Meanwhile, mix together all the ingredients of the vinaigrette.
3. Place ⅓ cup of vinaigrette with the chicken breasts in a resealable bag. Toss to coat.
4. Toss potatoes, mushrooms, beans, and onion with remaining vinaigrette. Set aside.
5. Grill the chicken breast until it is done. On a charcoal grill it will take about ten minutes per side.
6. Slice the grilled chicken breasts into thin strips. Divide the chicken and salad ingredients into four equal parts. Top with cherry tomatoes and serve.

Kebabs of Monkfish Wrapped in Bacon

⊙ SERVES 4 ⊙ PREPARATION TIME: ⊙ COOKING TIME:
1 hour 10 minutes 10 minutes
⊙ COST: DIFFICULTY:
Expensive Easy

1. Trim the fish and curl it into chunks about 2 in./5 cm square. Put into a bowl with the rind and juice of the lemon, rosemary, olive oil, and crushed green peppercorns. Cover and put in the fridge for an hour.

2. Remove the fish from the fridge and then wrap each chunk in strips of bacon. Reserve the marinade. Thread the chunks onto the skewers.

3. Brush the kebabs with a little olive oil and then cook over a medium barbecue for ten minutes, basting with the marinade and turning while cooking.

- ⊙ 1 lb 6 oz/700 g monkfish fillets
- ⊙ juice and grated rind of 1 lemon
- ⊙ a few sprigs of fresh rosemary
- ⊙ 3 tbsp olive oil
- ⊙ ½ tsp green peppercorns, crushed
- ⊙ 8-10 strips of thinly sliced streaky bacon
- ⊙ wooden skewers soaked in water for 30 minutes

Sardines with Lemon Salsa

- 12-16 fresh sardines
- olive oil
- juice of 1 lemon

FOR THE SALSA:
- 1 preserved lemon or 1 whole lemon previously frozen and then thawed
- 1 tbsp olive oil
- 1 red onion finely chopped
- 1 clove of garlic, crushed
- 1 tsp coriander seed, crushed
- 4 small tomatoes, finely chopped
- 1 tsp brown sugar
- 2 tbsp fresh parsley, chopped
- 2 tbsp fresh coriander, chopped
- salt and freshly ground black pepper

- SERVES 4
- PREPARATION TIME: 5 minutes
- COOKING TIME: 5-6 minutes
- COST: Low
- DIFFICULTY: Easy

1. Clean the fish, then dry with kitchen paper.
2. Make the salsa by finely chopping the lemon, discarding the seeds. Heat the olive oil in a pan over a medium heat. Add the onion, garlic, and coriander seed and cook for 3-4 minutes until soft. Take off the heat and stir in the lemon and the rest of the ingredients and mix well. Keep warm until the sardines are cooked.
3. Brush the sardines with oil and lemon juice. Cook on the barbecue over a medium heat for two minutes on each side. Serve with the salsa.

Seared Tuna Niçoise Salad

⊙ SERVES 4 ⊙ PREPARATION TIME: ⊙ COOKING TIME:
2 hours 20 minutes 15 minutes

⊙ COST: DIFFICULTY:
Reasonable Tricky

1. Put the tuna into a shallow dish. Mix together the olive oil, lemon rind and juice, and black pepper and pour over the steaks. Cover and place in the fridge for two hours.

2. Trim the beans and put into plenty of boiling, salted water. Bring back to the boil and cook for 4-5 minutes until tender. Drain and rinse in cold water and set to one side.

3. Cook the potatoes in the same way for 10-15 minutes. Drain and cut into small chunks. Cook the eggs in boiling water for 8-10 minutes. Drain and put into cold water.

4. Arrange the beans, potatoes, red onion, tomatoes, and anchovies on plates. Peel the eggs and cut each into quarters and place one egg on each plate. Mix together the dressing ingredients.

5. Drain the tuna steaks and cook them on a high heat for about eight minutes, turning once. Place one steak on the top of each plate and then drizzle the dressing on top before serving.

INGREDIENTS

⊙ 4 6 oz/170 g tuna steaks
⊙ grated rind and juice of 1 lemon
⊙ 2 tbsp olive oil
⊙ freshly ground black pepper

FOR THE SALAD:
⊙ 12 oz/350 g fine French beans
⊙ 12 small new potatoes
⊙ 4 eggs
⊙ 1 small red onion cut into very fine rings
⊙ 4 large tomatoes cut into chunks
⊙ 4-6 anchovies from a tin cut into thin strips
⊙ 4 tbsp olive oil
⊙ 1 clove of garlic, crushed
⊙ juice of 1 lemon
⊙ a dash of chili sauce
⊙ a pinch of sugar
⊙ salt and freshly ground black pepper

73

- 24 oysters in their shells
- 4-5 red chilies finely chopped
- white wine vinegar
- olive oil
- hot pepper sauce
- zest of 1 fresh lime
- juice of 1 fresh lemon
- rock salt

Oysters with Chili and Lime

- SERVES 4-6
- PREPARATION TIME: 20 minutes
- COOKING TIME: 2-3 minutes
- COST: Expensive
- DIFFICULTY: Low

1. Shell the fresh oysters. Remove the top part of each shell, leaving the live oyster in the bottom part.
2. Finely chop the red chilies, and mix together in a bowl with the white wine vinegar, olive oil, hot pepper sauce, lemon juice, salt, and the zest of a lime.
3. Drizzle the dressing onto each oyster.
4. Place the oysters on the grill over very hot coals for 2-3 minutes. Serve immediately.

Barbecued Lobster with Lime and Chili Butter

⊙ SERVES 6 ⊙ PREPARATION TIME: ⊙ COOKING TIME:
10 minutes 8-9 minutes

⊙ COST: DIFFICULTY:
Expensive Tricky

FOR THE BUTTER:
- 4 oz/100 g butter, softened
- juice and grated rind of 1 lime
- 1 red chili, deseeded and very finely chopped

- 3 1½ lb/750 g uncooked lobsters
- 2 lemons, cut into quarters
- salt and freshly ground black pepper

1. Mix the butter with the lime juice, rind and the chili. Form into a cylinder, place in plastic wrap and put into the fridge to harden.

2. Prepare the lobsters by cutting each one in half lengthwise along the back of the shell. Remove the long dark vein, and crack the claws.

3. Squeeze a little lemon juice onto the flesh, sprinkle with salt and pepper, and put the lobsters flesh-side down on a medium barbecue. Turn over after one minute and cook for another 7-8 minutes until the flesh is white and the shells are red. Put some slices of the lime and chili butter on top of the lobster flesh and allow to melt slightly. Then remove from the barbecue and serve with the lemon quarters.

- 4 trout, cleaned and gutted
- 2 cloves of garlic, cut in half
- 1 large lemon, cut into thin slices
- 4 sprigs fresh thyme
- salt and freshly ground black pepper
- olive oil

Trout over Coals

⊙ SERVES 4 ⊙ PREPARATION TIME: ⊙ COOKING TIME:
10 minutes 12-15 minutes
⊙ COST: DIFFICULTY:
Reasonable Easy

1. Prepare the trout by rubbing the cavities with the garlic cloves. Put lemon slices, thyme, salt and pepper, and a little olive oil into each cavity.

2. Brush four pieces of tinfoil with olive oil and place a trout on each one. Brush the trout with more olive oil. Put the trout on the foil onto a medium barbecue and cook for 12-15 minutes, turning once during the cooking time.

Grilled Pork Steaks with Lemon Butter Sauce

INGREDIENTS

- 3 tbsp butter
- 2 tsp lemon juice
- 1 clove of garlic, crushed
- 6 pork chops
- 1 pinch salt

⊙ SERVES 6

⊙ PREPARATION TIME:
10 minutes

⊙ COOKING TIME:
20 minutes

⊙ COST:
Low

⊙ DIFFICULTY:
Easy

1. Preheat an outdoor grill to a high heat and lightly oil the grate.

2. Melt the butter in a small saucepan over a medium heat.
   Stir in the lemon juice and the garlic and heat until the garlic
   is tender. Then remove from the heat.

3. Arrange the chops on a plate and coat the top side of each
   one with the butter mixture. Place the chops on the grill,
   butter side down.

4. Sear over a high heat for one minute, coating the top side of
   the chops with the butter mixture while the other side is
   grilling. Flip the chops and sear the other side for one minute.

5. Turn the meat, cover the grill and cook for 3-5 minutes per
   side, brushing occasionally with any butter mixture left over.
   Add salt to season.

- 5 lb/2.2 kg
  pork spare ribs
- 4 oz/125 g butter
- 1 onion, chopped
- 1 tbsp
  crushed garlic
- ½ cup distilled
  white wine vinegar
- 13 tbsp/230 ml water
- 3 tbsp tomato sauce
- 3 tbsp hickory
  smoke-flavored
  barbecue sauce
- 1 lemon, juiced
- salt and pepper to taste

Barbecued Pork Ribs

- ⊙ SERVES 4
- ⊙ PREPARATION TIME:
  2 hours 20 minutes
- ⊙ COST:
  Low
- ⊙ COOKING TIME:
  1 hour 20 minutes
  DIFFICULTY:
  Easy

1. Place the ribs in a large frying pan. Cover with salted water and bring to the boil. Reduce the heat, and allow the ribs to simmer for one hour, or until the meat is tender. Remove from the heat and drain.

2. Melt the butter in a saucepan and sauté the onion and garlic until the onion is tender. Remove from heat. Put the water, wine vinegar, tomato sauce, barbecue sauce, and lemon juice in a blender. Season with salt and pepper and pour in the melted butter mixture. Purée for one minute, then pour back in saucepan. Bring to a boil, then remove from the heat.

3. Place the boiled ribs in a shallow baking dish and pour the sauce all over them. Place in the refrigerator for two hours.

4. Barbecue the ribs on a grill over moderately hot coals, basting with the sauce and turning often until well browned.

Skewered Pork with Mushrooms

⊙ SERVES 4   ⊙ PREPARATION TIME: ⊙ COOKING TIME:
              15 minutes   15-20 minutes
              ⊙ COST: DIFFICULTY:
              Reasonable   Average

1. Cut the meat into 1 in./2.5 cm square cubes and place in a
   large mixing bowl together with the garlic, olive oil, salt,
   and pepper. Mix well.
2. Thread onto four skewers, alternating the pork with the bay
   leaves and mushrooms.
3. Cook over hot coals for 15-20 minutes, turning occasionally
   and basting with the remaining oil. Serve immediately.

INGREDIENTS

⊙ 1 lb/450 g pork fillet
⊙ 4 tbsp olive oil
⊙ 2 cloves of garlic, crushed
⊙ salt and black pepper
⊙ 24 button mushrooms
⊙ 24 fresh bay leaves

Honey Mustard Pork Chops

- 4 pork chops,
  about 3/4 in./2 cm thick

FOR THE MARINADE:
- 6 tbsp/90 ml honey
- 3 tbsp fresh orange juice
- 1 tbsp cider vinegar
- 1 tbsp white wine
- 2 tsp Worcestershire sauce
- 2 tsp onion powder
- 1/2 tsp dried tarragon
- 3 tbsp Dijon mustard

⊙ SERVES 4 ⊙ PREPARATION TIME: ⊙ COOKING TIME:
2 hours 10 minutes 25-30 minutes
⊙ COST: DIFFICULTY:
Low Easy

1. In a small bowl, mix together the honey, orange juice, cider vinegar, white wine, Worcestershire sauce, onion powder, tarragon, and mustard.

2. Slash the fatty edge of each chop in 4-5 places, without cutting into the meat, to prevent the meat curling during cooking. Place the chops in a shallow dish then cover with the marinade. Refrigerate for two hours.

3. Grill the chops over medium hot coals for 12-15 minutes each side, turning three or four times and basting with the remaining marinade, or until done.

Boned Leg of Lamb with Mint Raita

⊙ SERVES 4 ⊙ PREPARATION TIME: 8 hours 30 minutes ⊙ COOKING TIME: 16-20 minutes

⊙ COST: Dear

DIFFICULTY: Average

1. Mix together the marinade ingredients. Put the lamb in a shallow dish, pour over the marinade, thoroughly coating the lamb. Cover and leave in a cool place for anything up to eight hours.

2. Put all the ingredients for the raita into a bowl and mix well. Keep in a cool place until the lamb is cooked.

3. Remove the lamb from the marinade and cook over a medium heat for 8-10 minutes on each side, turning once. Cut the lamb into thick slices, serving with the raita for dipping.

INGREDIENTS

⊙ 1 lb 12 oz/950 g boned half leg of lamb

FOR THE MARINADE:
⊙ 3 tbsp olive oil
⊙ juice of ½ a lemon
⊙ 1 clove of garlic, crushed
⊙ 1 tbsp fresh chopped rosemary
⊙ 1 tsp dried oregano
⊙ freshly ground black pepper

FOR THE MINT RAITA:
⊙ 1 lb/450 g Greek yogurt
⊙ 2 cloves of garlic, crushed
⊙ 2 tsp dried mint
⊙ 1 tbsp fresh chopped parsley
⊙ salt and freshly ground black pepper

INGREDIENTS

- 1 lb 2 oz/500 g minced lamb
- 1 onion, finely chopped
- 2 cloves of garlic, crushed
- 1 tsp dried oregano
- a pinch of mild chili powder
- 1 tsp Dijon mustard
- salt and freshly ground black pepper
- 2 oz/50 g crumbled feta cheese
- 1 tsp dried mint
- olive oil

Lamb Burgers with Feta

⊙ SERVES 4   ⊙ PREPARATION TIME:
                10 minutes
              ⊙ COST:
                Low

⊙ COOKING TIME:
   10 minutes
   DIFFICULTY:
   Average

1. Use your hands to mix the lamb with the onion, garlic, oregano, chili powder, and mustard. Season with salt and black pepper. Divide into eight portions and shape into flattened rounds.

2. Mix the feta cheese with the dried mint. Put a little of the feta into the center of four of the rounds. Put another round on top of each and shape into four burgers.

3. Brush the burgers with olive oil and cook on a medium barbecue for about ten minutes, turning once.

Lamb Shish Kebabs

⊙ SERVES 4 ⊙ PREPARATION TIME: ⊙ COOKING TIME:
2 hours 10 minutes 10 minutes

⊙ COST: DIFFICULTY:
Reasonable Average

1. Cut the lamb into 1 in./2.5 cm cubes. In a large bowl, mix together the olive oil, garlic, balsamic vinegar, harissa or chili powder, and salt and black pepper. Add the lamb and coat well. Cover and put in the fridge for two hours.

2. Drain the lamb and reserve the marinade. Thread the lamb cubes onto the skewers, alternating with the tomatoes, mushrooms, peppers, and basil leaves. Brush with the marinade and cook on a hot barbecue for ten minutes, turning during the cooking and basting with a little extra olive oil.

⊙ 8 oz/225 g boned leg of lamb
⊙ 2 tbsp olive oil
⊙ 1 clove of garlic, crushed
⊙ 1 tsp balsamic vinegar
⊙ a pinch of harissa or mild chili powder
⊙ salt and freshly ground black pepper
⊙ 8 cherry tomatoes
⊙ 8-12 button mushrooms
⊙ 2 small green peppers, cut into small chunks
⊙ a handful of fresh basil leaves
⊙ extra olive oil for basting
⊙ 4 metal or wooden skewers, soaked in water for 30 minutes

Lamb Tikka Kebabs

- 1 lb/450 g shoulder or neck fillet of lamb cut into 1 in./2.5 cm cubes
- 5 oz/150 g natural yogurt
- 1 clove of garlic, crushed
- 1tbsp ground coriander
- juice of 1 lemon
- 2 tsp chopped fresh parsley
- 1 tsp turmeric
- 1 tsp chili powder
- 1 tsp garam masala
- 4 metal or wooden skewers, soaked in water for 30 minutes

⊙ SERVES 4 ⊙ PREPARATION TIME: 4 hours 20 minutes ⊙ COOKING TIME: 10-15 minutes

⊙ COST: Reasonable DIFFICULTY: Average

1. Divide the cubed lamb into four servings. Then spear onto wooden skewers and place in a shallow bowl.

2. Mix together all the other ingredients to form a marinade.

3. Spoon the marinade over the meat, cover, and marinate in the fridge for four hours.

4. Cook for 10-15 minutes on a pre-heated barbecue, turning frequently and brushing with the spare marinade.

Halloumi and Zucchini Kebabs

⊙ SERVES 8 ⊙ PREPARATION TIME: ⊙ COOKING TIME:
3 hours 10 minutes   5-7 minutes

⊙ COST: ⊙ DIFFICULTY:
Low   Average

1. Put the olive oil, dried mint, garlic, lime or lemon juice and salt and black pepper into a large bowl and mix well. Cut the zucchinis into slices about 1/3 in./1 cm thick, slice the cherry tomatoes in half and cut the halloumi cheese into 3/4 in./2 cm square small chunks. Put everything into the bowl and mix well. Cover and leave in the fridge for up to three hours.

2. When ready to cook, thread the zucchinis, tomatoes, and cheese onto the skewers, putting a couple of basil leaves on each between the vegetables and cheese. Brush each kebab with a little of the marinade and then cook on a hot barbecue for 5-7 minutes, turning and basting while cooking.

INGREDIENTS

⊙ 3 tbsp olive oil
⊙ 2 tsp dried mint
⊙ 1 clove of garlic, crushed
⊙ juice of 1 lime or lemon
⊙ salt and freshly ground black pepper
⊙ 6 small zucchinis
⊙ about 16 cherry tomatoes
⊙ 250 g/10 oz halloumi cheese
⊙ a handful of fresh basil leaves
⊙ 8 wooden skewers soaked in water for 30 minutes

97

Peppers Stuffed with Lemon Risotto

- 4 red or yellow peppers
- 2 tsp olive oil
- 4 oz/100 g arborio or short grain rice, cooked and drained
- 1 tbsp red pesto sauce
- 2 tbsp toasted pine nuts
- juice of 1 lemon
- 2 tbsp fresh chopped parsley
- salt and freshly ground black pepper
- A few shavings of Parmesan cheese

⊙ SERVES 4 ⊙ PREPARATION TIME: 10 minutes

⊙ COOKING TIME: 30 minutes

⊙ COST: Reasonable

DIFFICULTY: Easy

1. Cut the peppers in half through the stalk. Remove the seeds and stalk. Brush with olive oil and cook on a medium barbecue for fifteen minutes or until soft.
2. Mix the cooked rice with the pesto sauce, pine nuts, lemon juice, parsley, and salt and black pepper. Put some of the rice mixture into each pepper half. Top with one or two shavings of Parmesan cheese and drizzle with olive oil.
3. Put back on the barbecue for another fifteen minutes.

Aubergine and Pepper Parmesan Sandwiches

⊙ SERVES 4   ⊙ PREPARATION TIME: ⊙ COOKING TIME:
                    15 minutes   10 minutes

              ⊙ COST: ⊙ DIFFICULTY:
                Reasonable   Easy

1. Preheat your barbecue.
2. Place the aubergine and red bell pepper on the barbecue, and season with salt and pepper. Cook for 5-10 minutes, until tender and slightly browned.
3. Cut the baguette in half lengthwise. Spread goat's cheese on the bottom half, followed by tapenade. Layer with aubergine and red pepper, then sprinkle with Parmesan cheese. Cover with the top half of the baguette. Cut into four pieces. Serve hot or cold.

Portobello Mushroom Sandwiches

- 2 cloves of garlic, crushed
- 6 tbsp olive oil
- ½ tsp dried thyme
- 2 tbsp balsamic vinegar
- salt and pepper to taste
- 4 large portobello mushroom caps
- 4 hamburger buns
- 2 tbsp mayonnaise
- 1 tbsp capers, drained
- 1 large tomato, sliced
- 4 lettuce leaves

⊙ SERVES 4   ⊙ PREPARATION TIME: ⊙ COOKING TIME:
8 minutes   9 minutes
⊙ COST: DIFFICULTY:
Very low   Easy

1. In a medium-size mixing bowl, mix together the garlic, olive oil, thyme, vinegar, salt, and pepper.
2. Brush the mushroom caps with the dressing and place, bottom side up, onto the barbecue.
3. Turn the caps and continue cooking.
4. In a small bowl, mix the capers and mayonnaise. Spread the mayonnaise mixture on the buns, top with mushroom caps, tomato, and lettuce.

Beef Marinade

⊙ SERVES
12

⊙ PREPARATION TIME:
6 hours 5 minutes

⊙ COOKING TIME:
None

⊙ COST:
Reasonable

⊙ DIFFICULTY:
Easy

1. In a medium bowl, stir together the soy sauce, vinegar, olive oil, orange juice, ginger, garlic, mustard, and brown sugar.

2. Pour the marinade over the beef in a shallow container, making sure all the meat is submerged.

3. Cover and refrigerate for at least six hours.

⊙ 6 fl oz/185 ml soy sauce
⊙ 2 fl oz/60 ml rice wine vinegar
⊙ 3 fl oz/80 ml olive oil
⊙ 3 fl oz/80 ml orange juice
⊙ 2 tbsp crushed fresh ginger root
⊙ 2 tbsp crushed garlic
⊙ 1½ tbsp ground mustard
⊙ 1½ tbsp brown sugar

Delicious Barbecue Sauce

INGREDIENTS

- 1 (12 fl oz) can cola-flavored carbonated beverage
- 8 tbsp tomato sauce
- ½ finely chopped onion
- 1 clove of garlic
- ½ tsp hot pepper sauce

- SERVES
  6

- PREPARATION TIME:
  5 minutes
- COST:
  Low

- COOKING TIME:
  20 minutes
  DIFFICULTY:
  Easy

1. In a medium saucepan, combine the cola, tomato sauce, onion, garlic, and hot pepper sauce.
2. Cook over a medium heat until reduced by a third and thickened.

West Indian Barbecue Sauce

⊙ SERVES
12

⊙ PREPARATION TIME:
1 hour 5 minutes

⊙ COOKING TIME:
None

⊙ COST:
Reasonable

⊙ DIFFICULTY:
Average

1. Combine the green onions, shallots, garlic, ginger, allspice, ground black pepper, chili peppers, cinnamon, nutmeg, salt, brown sugar, orange juice, vinegar, wine, soy sauce, oil, and molasses in a bowl.

2. Mix well, cover and allow to sit for an hour.

3. Mix well again before adding to fish or meat. Throw away any leftover sauce.

⊙ 6 green onions, chopped
⊙ 3 tbsp finely chopped shallots
⊙ 2 cloves of garlic, crushed
⊙ 1 tsp ground ginger
⊙ 1 tbsp ground allspice
⊙ 1 tsp ground black pepper
⊙ 2 chili peppers, chopped
⊙ 1 tsp ground cinnamon
⊙ 1/2 tsp ground nutmeg
⊙ 1 tsp salt
⊙ 1 tbsp brown sugar
⊙ 4 fl oz/125 ml fresh orange juice
⊙ 4 fl oz/125 ml cider vinegar
⊙ 2 fl oz/60 ml red wine
⊙ 2 fl oz/60 ml soy sauce
⊙ 2 fl oz/60 ml vegetable oil
⊙ 1 tbsp molasses

A Traditional Marinade

- 2½ fl oz/80 ml Worcestershire sauce
- 4 oz/125 g brown sugar
- juice of two lemons
- 4 oz/125 g butter, melted
- 4 tbsp red wine vinegar
- ¼ tsp onion powder
- ¼ tsp garlic powder
- ¼ tsp salt
- ½ tsp ground black pepper

⊙ SERVES 8 ⊙ PREPARATION TIME: 5 minutes ⊙ COOKING TIME: 5 minutes

⊙ COST: Reasonable DIFFICULTY: Average

1. In a medium bowl, combine the Worcestershire sauce, brown sugar, lemon juice, butter, vinegar, onion powder, garlic powder, salt, and ground black pepper.
2. Mix together well and pour over whichever meat you fancy.

Grilled Amaretti Peaches

⊙ SERVES 4 ⊙ PREPARATION TIME: ⊙ COOKING TIME:
        5 minutes   5-7 minutes
        ⊙ COST: ⊙ DIFFICULTY:
        Low   Very easy

1. Cut the peaches in half and remove the stones, scooping out the centers slightly with a teaspoon.
2. Cream the butter until soft and mix in the amaretti biscuits.
3. Put a little of the mixture into the hollow in the center of each peach. Sprinkle with demerara sugar.
4. Cook the peach halves on a hot barbecue for 5-7 minutes or until they start to soften.

- 4 ripe peaches
- 2 oz/50 g unsalted butter
- 8 small amaretti biscuits, crushed
- 2 oz/50 g demerara sugar

Plum and Cinnamon Toast

- 2 English muffins or
  4 slices of brioche
- 8 large ripe plums
- 2 oz/50 g
  unsalted butter
- 1 oz/25 g caster sugar
- ½ tsp ground cinnamon
- crème fraîche

⊙ SERVES 4 ⊙ PREPARATION TIME: ⊙ COOKING TIME:
  5 minutes 8-10 minutes
  ⊙ COST: DIFFICULTY:
  Reasonable Average

1. Slice the muffins in half. If using brioche, cut out four
   circles about 3 in./7.5 cm in diameter. Toast the muffins cut
   side down, or the brioche very lightly on one side, on a
   medium barbecue. Remove from the heat.

2. Slice the plums in half, remove the stones, and cut into
   slices. Cream the butter with the sugar and cinnamon.
   Spread a little onto the toasted side of the muffins or
   brioche. Top with a few slices of plum and dot with the rest
   of the butter mixture. Put back onto the barbecue to grill
   the underside for another 2-3 minutes until the butter on
   top of the plums has melted. Serve with crème fraîche.

Baked Bananas with Chocolate and Spiced Crème Fraîche

⊙ SERVES 4 ⊙ PREPARATION TIME: 5 minutes ⊙ COOKING TIME: 5 minutes

⊙ COST: Cheap ⊙ DIFFICULTY: Easy

INGREDIENTS

- ⊙ 4 large firm bananas
- ⊙ 1 oz/50 g plain chocolate, finely chopped
- ⊙ 1 oz/50 g demerara sugar
- ⊙ 8½ oz/250 ml crème fraîche
- ⊙ ½ tsp ground cinnamon
- ⊙ grated rind and juice of 1 orange

1. Cut the bananas along one side using a sharp knife, opening the skin enough to cut into the banana flesh to make a slit. Put a little of the chocolate into each slit and then sprinkle with the demerara sugar. Put the bananas onto a hot barbecue, cut side up, for five minutes or so, until the skins turn black.

2. Mix the crème fraîche with the cinnamon, rind, and juice of the orange.

3. Remove the bananas from the heat and slit open the skins completely. Serve straight away with the crème fraîche.

Fruit Compote

- ⊙ 5 small, ripe peaches, quartered and pitted
- ⊙ 6 small, ripe plums, quartered and pitted
- ⊙ 8½ fl oz/250 ml water
- ⊙ 6½ fl oz/185 ml orange-flavored liqueur
- ⊙ 7 fl oz/200 g sugar
- ⊙ zest of 1 lemon
- ⊙ 2 tsp pure vanilla extract
- ⊙ vanilla frozen yogurt (optional)

⊙ SERVES 5

⊙ PREPARATION TIME:
5 minutes

⊙ COST:
Low

⊙ COOKING TIME:
2 hours 20 minutes

DIFFICULTY:
Tricky

1. Place the fruit pieces in the center of the barbecue. Cook for 4-6 minutes, turning once. When the fruit is warmed through, remove and set to one side.

2. Combine water, liqueur, and sugar in a saucepan and bring to the boil. Meanwhile, cut the zest from the lemon and add it in strips to the pan, along with the vanilla. Continue boiling for about fifteen minutes, until liquid is reduced and syrupy.

3. Transfer the syrup to a serving bowl. Cut grilled fruit into bite-size pieces, add to the syrup and stir. Chill for at least two hours to allow fruits to absorb the flavor of the syrup. Compote may be prepared a day in advance and kept in the refrigerator overnight.

4. Serve compote with a little of the syrup spooned over the frozen yogurt.

Daiquiri (original)

⊙ SERVES 1 ⊙ PREPARATION TIME: ⊙ DIFFICULTY:
5 minutes Easy

⊙ COST:
Expensive

Method

Combine all the ingredients together in a cocktail shaker.

Shake with ice and strain into a highball glass over fresh ice.

Garnish

Serve with a twisted slice of lime or serve in a sugar-frosted glass.

INGREDIENTS

⊙ 1.7 fl oz/50 ml
golden rum
⊙ 0.4 fl oz/12.5 ml fresh
lime juice
⊙ 0.4 fl oz/12.5 ml
sugar syrup

- 1.7 fl oz/50 ml golden rum
- 0.8 fl oz/25 ml cream
- 1.7 fl oz/50 ml pineapple juice

Pina Colada

- SERVES 1
- PREPARATION TIME: 5 minutes
- DIFFICULTY: Easy
- COST: Expensive

Method

Shake all the ingredients with ice in a cocktail shaker and strain over ice into a highball glass.

Garnish

Serve with a pineapple wedge and a cocktail umbrella.

Moscow Mule

⊙ SERVES 1 ⊙ PREPARATION TIME: ⊙ DIFFICULTY:
            5 minutes   Easy

            ⊙ COST:
               Expensive

Method

Fill a highball glass with ice and pour in the vodka, followed by the lime juice, then the ginger beer.

Garnish

Serve with a wedge of lime and sugar-frost the glass for effect.

INGREDIENTS

⊙ 1.7 fl oz/50 ml vodka
⊙ 0.8 fl oz/25 ml
   fresh lime
⊙ ginger beer

Long Island Iced Tea

⊙ 0.4 fl oz/12.5 ml vodka
⊙ 0.4 fl oz/12.5 ml gin
⊙ 0.4 fl oz/12.5 ml
  white rum
⊙ 0.4 fl oz/12.5 ml tequila
⊙ 0.4 fl oz/12.5 ml
  triple sec
⊙ 0.8 fl oz/25 ml fresh
  lemon juice
⊙ 2 dashes of gomme syrup
⊙ cola-flavoured
  carbonated beverage

⊙ SERVES 2 ⊙ PREPARATION TIME: ⊙ DIFFICULTY:
              10 minutes   Average
            ⊙ COST:
              Expensive

Method

Combine the vodka, gin, white rum, tequila, triple sec, and lemon juice in a cocktail shaker with ice.

Add a dash of gomme syrup in each glass with some fresh ice.

Share out the shaken cocktail into each glass, then top up with cola.

Garnish

Serve with a slice of lime and a straw.

Conclusion

Barbecues are a great way to entertain family and friends, partly because anyone who wants to be involved can be. What's more, the food can be simple or elaborate—it's up to you. A barbecue can turn the simplest of dishes, a steak, a fillet of fish, or even a burger, into something special.

The earthiness of cooking on an open fire is fundamentally appealing, as it puts people in touch with times past and also other cultures around the world. The smells, flavors and visions of food cooked in this way are without doubt a sizzling experience!